Cackle Goes to Florida

By
Mary Lamb Lucas

Illustrations By: Bibiana Rivero

DEDICATION

This book is dedicated to all the parents and their children who love to read or have stories read to them. Stories that fill the imagination and create joy for all who hear them and read them.

Acknowledgments

No book would ever be published without the helpful writer friends, writing workshops such as Aspen Words where I met writers, editors, and many teachers of writing workshops. I am forever grateful to all of them and to all of my writing friends who read parts or all of this book and encouraged it forward. People like Holly Proctor, the "general encourager" in my neighborhood, who even shared an excerpt from Cackle in the neighborhood magazine.

October's ochre hue had begun to paint the rolling countryside of the middle reaches of the James River in Virginia. Cackle soared and floated on the day's thin currents, lost in a recurring reverie. She was an old crow, so old that no one in her flock could remember a time when she wasn't there. Her mate, Crazy Foot, told her that her feathers were looking shabby and rumpled. He wanted her to have them trimmed and shined up, but she didn't have time for such foolishness. She wanted to go to Florida. She was tired of the damp, cold winters in Virginia. Even though she didn't want Crazy Foot to know, she felt that her feathers didn't keep her as warm as they had when she was younger. Her parents, grandparents, great-grandparents, and other older crows used to say that Florida was the land of warm sunshine. None of them had been, as far as she knew, but all were sure that someone before them had firsthand knowledge. The legend had been passed down and become part of flock lore. It told of a fountain that enhanced life. Anyone could drink from it. It also said that there was a plentiful supply of food. It sounded good to Cackle and since she had done just about everything she had ever wanted except go to Florida, that's what she planned to do. She had not realized how much trouble it would be to get away. "You're too old to take such a flight. Do you know how far it is from Virginia to Florida?" said Crazy Foot.

"Do you know?" Asked Cackle.

"No." He said.

"I know that others have done it, and if they have, I can, too." Said Cackle. "I want you to come with me. We might want to stay."

"Why would I want to leave our nice home here and all our friends, children, and grandchildren? You may think you're a smart crow, but you have lost your mind! No. I'm not going, and you don't need to go, either," said Crazy Foot, turning his beak and looking away from Cackle. His own feathers, once so sleek and shiny, were dull and ruffled. He looked nothing like a descendant of the proud Crow tribe, yet he was. He was named for one of his ancestors.

Cackle loved Crazy Foot, but when he was obtuse and stubborn, she lost patience with him. He would never understand how much exploring meant to her. On the contrary, he was content to remain where he'd been hatched. A gypsy life had no appeal for him.

The Flock Council came, asking Cackle to please reconsider. They needed her to keep the flock together. She was an expert teacher of scouting, although she thought that stealth was her true gift. She knew all the ways there were to evade human hunters and other predators such as owls and hawks. Most of all, she was a leader. Everyone in the flock looked to her for guidance. "How," asked Ruby, the Council Co-Head, "can you even consider leaving us? This flock depends on you. I depend on you to be my friend. Who will chase Hawks with me? Who will play tricks on humans with me? You have to stay here!" "I have to go," Cackle said.

Soon, a number of the teenagers came to her, begging and pleading with her not to go.

"You haven't finished teaching us all we need to know," they said.

"If you came with me, I could continue teaching you," said Cackle.

"Come with you?" They said in one voice, "Our parents would never let us do that. They think it's a crazy idea."

"What do they know? They've never tried it," said Cackle.

"If you'll pardon me for being so bold," said Percy, one of the teenagers who was very respectful of his elders, "have you been there?"

"Of course not, that's why I want to go," said Cackle. "I want to see for myself."

"But how long will it take you to get there?" They asked.

"As long as it takes," replied Cackle.

"What will you eat along the way?" They said.

"Food, of course," said Cackle.

"But how do you know you'll find anything? We know where to look here. You don't know anything about where you're going?" They said.

"I do know that I'm a good spotter," said Cackle, "and if I can do that here, I can do it wherever I am."

"I think it sounds exciting," said Swooper, hopping up and down, "I wish I could go with you."

"You can," said Cackle. "I'd be glad to have your company."

"Excuse me," said Percy, "but where will you roost if you are far away from home?"

"I'll consult other flocks along the way and trust my instincts," said Cackle.

"I'm going with you!" Said Swooper. Several of the others said they were, too, but some were afraid to consider such a thing and flew away to tell their parents.

Later, Ruby and Lucky, another Council member, joined Cackle on the branch where she was resting. They pleaded with her to rethink this foolish plan of going to Florida. They mentioned all the reasons why she shouldn't go. She knew nothing about how long it would take or about weather, food, roost locations, and dangerous enemies who might exist on the flyway. She didn't know the way, and, most of all, she didn't know if there really was such a thing as Florida.

"I'm sure there is a Florida, and I'm not afraid to fly into unknown territory. I'll ask other flocks along the way for directions if I need them." Said Cackle. "I know two things: one, Florida is south of here; two, I'm going."

That night, Crazy Foot didn't come to roost beside Cackle until after dark. When she said, "Good night," he was silent except for a faint chortle and click of his beak. In the morning, Cackle looked at Crazy Foot and said, "I don't want to leave you. I want you to come with me, but if you don't, I'm going anyway."

"I've never wanted to go anywhere else but here," said Crazy Foot. "What about our family and flock we would be leaving behind?"

"I think many of them are coming with us"', said Cackle. If you come, maybe all of them will, too."

"I don't know if I can even think about such a thing. When are you going?" Asked Crazy Foot.

"Soon. Tomorrow or the next day." Said Cackle. "I have to get rid of all the things I'm not taking and fly around for one last look in case I don't come back."

"Don't come back?" Said Crazy Foot.

"I might want to stay." Said Cackle.

Crazy Foot pointed his beak toward the sky with a quiet click and said what sounded like "chuff."

Cackle flew around all the next day, quickly sweeping out of her nest the bits and pieces of this and that: an acorn, a piece of corn cob, a dried-up worm that she had once wanted to preserve. She circled by some of her favorite places. She landed on the old shed roof at the corner of Brady's millet field, now a blanket of golden brown and pale green with a satiny wheat-colored binding made by the partially desiccated brush around the edges of the field. She glided toward the tall sycamore tree that overlooked the lush bottomland along Fox Creek, and she took a minute by the edge of farmer Talley's big corn field. "Memories," she thought, "are good, but making new ones is even better." Before sundown, she was ready to go.

"Who's going with me?" She asked.

A chorus of "I am, "Not me," "Maybe," and "Can I..." answered her back.

The teenagers, Swooper, and his pals, except for Percy, who was still waiting for permission from his parents, were going. Crazy Foot had not said yes or no. Ruby had surprised them all by saying she wanted to go, but provisions had to be made for her place on the Council. Percy's parents, Mildred and Gerald, said they were against the principle of the thing.

"Any flight out of home territory is an unnecessary risk," said Gerald. "And this one is unthinkable."

After many caks and caws, almost every crow in the flock had decided to join Cackle, but some were planning to sleep on it and make their final decision in the morning.

Cackle slept like a nestling and woke just before sunrise to a rustle in the roost that grew to a murmur and then to distinct, excited voices. One by one, each crow announced that he or she wanted to go to Florida, too, including Crazy Foot.

"We're going, but mind you, we're very skeptical about the whole undertaking. We are not at all sure that you know what you're doing, Cackle," said Gerald, speaking for his family.

"I know what I'm doing, but I don't know how it will turn out," said Cackle.

There was a slight nip in the air as the flock soared up to cruising altitude and headed south toward the river. The sky was a sparkling clear blue that always comes in October - a last burst of color before the ashen gray of November. Disparate conversations punctuated the movement of the birds as they jostled along in no distinct formation.

"Let's sing a song," said Swooper.

"Good idea", said Mamie. "What shall we sing? Let's sing a silly song! Let's make up a silly song!"

"Let's pick a tune, and everyone can take turns making up a line," said Swooper.

Cackle, ignoring Gerald's remark, flew toward an oak tree on the bank of the river. She landed on one of its branches, saying, "Time for a snack and a rest. I think we'll find something here." A flock of starlings appeared and confirmed that this was Hopewell, Virginia.

"Where are you headed?" Asked one of the starlings.

"Florida," said Cackle.

"Florida! Where is that?" Said a starling.

"South of here," said Cackle. "We want to see the sights along the way. What do you recommend?"

"The ocean!" Said one. "The beach!" Said another. "The Cape Hatteras Lighthouse!" A cacophony of crow and starling voices erupted, "Caw, caw, feeee, feeee." Each bird had something to say about the crows' itinerary. The young crows and starlings whirred excitedly over and around, doing aerial loops and dives. All except Percy, of course. He perched sedately on a branch alongside his parents, who preferred not to be part of the foolishness. Percy wanted to be with his friends but was still a little bit too timid to broach the subject with his parents.

"The Lighthouse sounds interesting," said Cackle.

"First, you must promise to stay the night with us and come to the square dance." Said the starling spokesman.

"A square dance!" said Cackle. "Of course, we'll stay for that.

A chorus of voices agreed. Back to the singing idea: they picked "O What a Beautiful Morning" for the tune.

"O, what a wonderful ringing

I have it in my magical ear. I've got a marvelous feeling

That it is a singing deer.

Zip eh dee do dah, zip eh dee ay."

The flock flew along, young ones singing and laughing at their own lyrics until suddenly, Percy started dropping down toward the ground. The flock circled back, calling to him. Mildred, his mother, flew down to him in a burst of speed, catching up with him just in time to prevent his collision with the ground. "What is the matter with you? You nearly crashed!" She said.

"I must've forgotten to flap my wings. I was having so much fun." Said Percy, giggling uncontrollably."

"Just proves the foolishness of this whole trip," Mildred said through a clenched beak. "I'm going to put a stop to it right now."

"No, no, please don't do that. I've never had so much fun in my life. You'll embarrass me if you complain. Please," he said.

"I'll think about it," said Mildred.

When they had caught up with the circling flock, Percy's cohorts began to tease him about forgetting to flap his wings, but it was good-natured, and he had never been happier. For the first time in his life, he felt like one of the gang.

They flew along, following the river's southeasterly course until they reached the edge of known territory.

"The Lighthouse sounds interesting," said Cackle.

"First, the square dance." Said the starling spokesman.

"Yes, the square dance!" Said Cackle. "Of course, we'll stay for that."

Once they had checked in at their roost, which was next to the Robert C. Byrd Motel, for the night, the flock set out to have some dinner and get ready for the square dance that was to be held at the fire station. They bustled about, washing their beaks and slicking their feathers back. Mamie, the liveliest young crow, wanted to have a bandana to wear around her neck. She swooshed away in search of a likely store, followed by Swooper, Percy, Penny, and a few others. Having found a Rose store, the young pals returned, decked out in colorful bandannas - red, purple, yellow, blue, aqua, pink - just in time for the dance.

The fire station was bustling with crows and starlings dressed in their square dance outfits. The males wore cowboy hats and shirts with bolo ties or bandannas. The females had on flouncy skirts in colors and styles that coordinated with each one's partner.

Crow feet began to tap and hop to the hoedown music being played by the musicians in the corner. "Come on," said Cackle, "let's get in squares!"

No sooner had she spoken than Slim, the caller, told everyone to find their partners and form squares.

"This is so exciting!" Crowed Mamie.

"Bow to your partner, then to your corner," drawled Slim as he began the call for the first dance.

"My left wing hurts," said Mildred.

"Look," said Crazy Foot to Cackle. "Look at Mamie and Percy. They're good at this."

Soon, they and Penny and Swooper stopped dancing to watch Mamie and Percy. A small crowd formed around their square.

Cries of "Way to go, Percy!" and "Yea, Mamie!" could be heard along with applause for their brilliant square dancing.

One dance after another seemed to fly by until Slim called the last dance a circle made up of all the crows and starlings, except for Budge, who was asleep inside a fiddle case. A chorus of "goodbyes" and "thank-yous" and promises from the crows to stop by another time echoed through the fire station. "Be careful on the way to the motel!" Said a starling. "Don't worry, we'll be fine." Said Cackle.

A flock of weary crows was flying low on their way to the motel when suddenly, Cackle shrieked, "Owl! Look out!" just as an owl swooped down toward one of the crows. It got its talons on Budge and was trying to lift him up. It all happened so fast. Budge's parents were in front of him chattering and didn't see or hear anything until Budge began to squeal - loud squeals.

First, Percy and Swooper flew at the owl, shrieking and squawking. Swooper attacked its face and beak. Percy went for a wing. When the owl loosened its hold on Budge, Percy flew under the startled Budge to catch and hold him until he remembered to fly. Then Percy joined Swooper and Cackle in chasing the owl away.

Mamie's voice rose above the general hubbub when she looked into Percy's eyes and said, "Percy, you were a hero!"

Lucky told Swooper that he, too, was a hero. "You helped save Budge's life tonight!" He said. "Come, let's all stop over there by that Poplar tree and catch our breath."

Upon landing, Ruby, speaking for herself and for the flock council, put her wings around both Percy and Swooper and thanked them for being so brave.

"Of course," she said, "We all have to thank Cackle's sharp eyes and quick wits for sounding the alert."

"Here, here," said Crazy Foot, obviously proud of his mate.

No one had noticed that Budge was now under the wing of his Father, Digger Man, with his head hanging down and tears in his eyes. He stayed there until he heard Mildred saying to Cackle, "None of this would have happened if YOU hadn't led us into this foolishness. We nearly lost Budge, Gerald and I ache all over; we're getting farther away from home, and who knows what might befall us next. I think we should go back."

"I th-i-nk," Budge said in a little voice that was froggy from fright and tears, "I think that we, that we ..... should go on."

There was silence for a moment and then cries of "Yay Budge!" and "On we go!" before someone started humming "Fly Like an Eagle." Except for Mildred, there seemed to be a consensus in favor of continuing to Florida.

"Remember," said Cackle, as her words were drowned by the rattle of chirps, caks, clucks, and caws from the flock before they flew to the motel for the night.

After breakfast the next morning, the flock conferred on safety tactics while a red-bellied woodpecker and a tufted titmouse watched. Cackle was impatient, but she waited for the others. When they finally took off, the titmouse and woodpecker called out, "Hope you enjoyed your stay! Come back! Good luck!"

Soaring once again brought back the flock's high spirits. Even Mildred and Gerald were silently elated. Everyone had decided to head for the Cape Hatteras lighthouse. They had no idea how far it was, but they knew it was along the coast. They flew and flew, and after a while, young ones could be heard asking, "What's that?" and "How much longer?"

More caks and caws continued as small groups within the flock conversed. There was an occasional burst of laughter or a loop de loop from Swooper and the other teenagers.

"Look, look!" Cried Budge, drawing the attention of the flock, "Cars are going into the water! Can they swim?"

Sure enough, a stream of cars at a place where the highway came to a big river was going down under the water. But then they could be seen coming up again on the other side.

"I think this is a tunnel for cars as groundhogs and foxes have," said Cackle. "But let's ask around. Why don't we fly over to that island and ask some of the seagulls?"

"Yes," said one of the seagulls, "that hole the cars disappear into is a tunnel that goes underneath the water. It's the Hampton Roads tunnel. You're at the mouth of the James River, where it empties into the Chesapeake Bay."

"This is exciting, said Budge in his high, squeaky voice, "Is this your home in the middle of all this water? Do you swim? Do you go in the tunnel, too? What's it like to live here? It's so windy. Are those ships? Where are they going? Have you ever been on one? "

"Slow down, young fella," said the seagull with a chuckle, "and I'll try to answer your questions. I don't live right here on this little island only but call the whole bay area my home. One night, I might sleep in a cove nearby and, by day, be back and forth between here and the beach out there. On other nights, I'm somewhere else. I've never been in the tunnel, but I know birds who have. I have landed on ships many times. People on them like to throw out food for us."

"They don't shoot at you? Asked Mamie."

"My goodness, no, why would they do that"? Said the gull.

"Well, they just do," said Mamie. "That's what they do to us. We always have to watch out for people with shotguns where we live."

"Hmm. They don't do that here", said the gull. "It's fun here in the summer when all the people come. They throw out food for us everywhere."

"Maybe we should live here," said Swooper.

"Maybe, said Cackle, but not until after we've been to Florida. Let's go, everyone! Enjoyed meeting you," she said to the gulls.

There were calls of "Thank you!" and "Goodbye!" back and forth between gulls and crows as the crows flew away.

"Just a minute! Just a minute! Gerald and I have something to say," said Mildred, causing crows to slow down and crane their necks at her.

"We don't like this drifting around, no itinerary for each day, no notion of what we're doing next, no reservations for the night, stopping on a whim. It's foolhardy and..and irresponsible! We think someone besides Cackle should be leading. If we're going to continue at all."

The flock was silent for a moment, and then all began talking at once. "Quiet!" Said Ruby. "Mildred, you are a stick-in-the-mud fussbudget! Either stop harping or go home!"

"But, but, phhhhh, you can't........." Gerald sputtered and then stopped, slowly and deliberately closing his beak. Mildred's beak was hanging open, unable to move.

"Yea, Ruby!" cried Swooper.

"Hear, hear!" Said most of the crows.

"It's ok, Percy, we don't blame you for how your parents are. We like you", said Mamie.

"You, you do?" said Percy. "I know my Mother can't help it, but she embarrasses me."

"Sometimes everyone's parents embarrass them," said Mamie.

"You always know how to say the right thing, Mamie. You're nice," said Percy.

"Hear, hear!" Said most of the crows.

"So are you, and you're brave, too," said Mamie. "Me? Brave?" Said Percy.

"Yes. How you helped to rescue Budge was heroic," she said.

"Oh, that," he said, blushing, "Look, we're getting behind. We should catch up!"

"Yikes! Watch out for the airplanes!" He said.

They had taken a turn south and were flying along the Atlantic coast near several airports and landing strips where planes were taking off and landing.

Soon, they were flying over the waters of Back Bay. Looking west, they could see the Great Dismal Swamp with its enormous, old trees. A pair of curious Canada Geese resting in the marshes of Back Bay flapped up to see what the flock of crows was doing there.

"Florida, eh?" said the gander. "It's a nice place. What's taking you there?" "You've been to Florida?" said Mamie.

"Yes, I've been there many times," said the gander.

"Percy, Swooper, everyone listen —he's been to Florida!" said Mamie.

The crows and the geese stopped in a grassy area near the water and introduced themselves to each other.

"I'm Cornwell, and this is my mate, Maisie, said the gander."

"Swooper," said Swooper, tipping his beak. "These are my friends, Mamie, Penny, Percy, and here come others," he said as he swept a wing out toward the gathering flock. "Cackle, here is why we're going to Florida."

"Hello, I'm Cackle," said Cackle. "I hear you've been to Florida."

"Yes, I have," said Cornwell."

"Oh yes, we stop there every year on our way to Mexico. It's lovely," said Maisie. "Although it is a bit crowded in places. We always enjoy the sun, the waterways, even the circus."

"The circus! There's a circus in Florida?" Said Cackle. "What's a circus?" Said Budge.

"So there really is a Florida," said Crazy Foot.

"The circus is amazing. They call it The Greatest Show on Earth," said Maisie in a rush, as if there wasn't enough time to tell it all. "There are animals, clowns, and acrobats performing in three rings at once. Florida is the home base for the Ringling Brothers Barnum & Bailey circus. It's where they have a school for clowns and one for trapeze artists, and I don't know what all. We love it, don't we, Cornie? So do our children and friends."

A hubbub of crow voices ensued as the older ones babbled about the news that these geese knew there was a Florida. The younger ones were excited about the circus. They were asking what animals, what's a trapeze, what's a clown?

When the talk subsided, Cackle asked the geese the best way to get to their destination. That made Mildred and Gerald happy.

Cornwell said, "Well, we more or less fly along the inland...."

"Waterway," said Maisie, "but sometimes we go along the coast and sometimes a good bit more inland. It depends on the weather. You can't miss it if you stay headed south."

"Why don't you come with us?" Said Mildred. "Then we'd be sure of getting there safely, that is, if you're going anyway."

"Oh yes! Do come with us!" Said a chorus of crows.

"That would be most unusual," said Cornwell in his deep voice, "though I'd like to help you." Maisie and I will have to think about that and talk with our flock. Can you stay a while, perhaps overnight, until we decide?"

"Yes, yes, of course we can," said Cackle and Ruby in unison as the others cawed their agreement. It was getting late in the day, and they needed to have a place for the night anyway. The crows flew around, investigating the area in their typical nosey way. The sea, with waves lapping on the shore and salty water, was new to them. Mamie and Swooper quickly made friends with some of the seagulls and other shore birds. Cackle was surprised to see no humans. She told Lucky that she was almost disappointed because she enjoyed trying to outwit them. They found a stand of trees suitable for the night that were beside Back Bay next to where the flock of geese were living. At dusk, when they settled down to roost, little murmurs, clicks, and chuffs wafted through the marshy air as the crows discussed their past two days.

"You have to admit," said Gerald to Mildred, "that so far we are all right."

"Only with a great deal of luck," said Mildred. "We almost lost Percy to his foolish fall and then Budge because we were out at night in unknown territory. Goodness knows what's next."

A few trees away, Percy was telling his pals that he was having the best time in his life, in spite of his parents' reservations and his tired wings. Swooper was looking forward to the days to come and feeling every moment more like a "crow of the world."

"Isn't it just the greatest? Imagine what tales we'll be able to tell our children and grandchildren!" Said Mamie. "We're making history!"

"I think I'm going to write a book about it," said Penny.

"Z z z z z z z z , chmpf, z z z z z z," was heard from Budge as his eyelids drooped down.

One by one, the others followed suit and let sleep enfold them. Strange new places dotted the landscapes of their dreams.

In the morning, Maisie and Cornwell told the crows that they would be able to go with them to Florida. They had discussed it with their flock and their children. The children were almost fully grown so it was a good opportunity for them to experience some time without their parents. The other geese thought that joining a flock of crows was irregular but gave their blessing. They would be flying south in a week or so, depending on the weather, and would join the pair on a farm pond they were familiar with outside of Tampa. The crows were glad to hear the news, especially Mildred and Gerald, who always preferred a sure thing.

There was quite a commotion as all the birds foraged for their breakfasts and then gathered to say goodbye to one another. The nearly grown goslings shed a tear or two as they said goodbye to their parents. Cornwell told them that he would miss them but that he was looking forward to hearing how well they had managed on their own. Mamie flitted here and there, saying goodbye and promising to stay in touch. All her friends, old and new, were friends for life. Swooper, too, flew around saying goodbye to each new friend he'd made. The seagulls, the terns, the geese, even a sand crab. Then he made a little speech to everyone gathered, thanking the geese for their hospitality and the loan of Maisie and Cornwell as guides, the other birds and crabs for sharing their home so graciously.

"Here, here," said Crazy Foot, flapping his wings together in agreement. The others joined him, cawing and flapping their gratitude and, at the same time, hopping up and down in their eagerness to be on their way. There was an unspoken new confidence within the flock regarding flying to Florida now that they had met the geese. Those who had doubted began to appreciate Cackle's vision and sense of adventure. Those who hadn't were even more excited. Again underway, they had become a flock of crows plus two geese whose movement was a fluttering banner that drew attention to the brilliant autumn sky. Cackle and Crazy Foot flew alongside Maisie and Cornwell, chit-chatting about this and that, mostly their families, like the two old longtime couples that they were.

When the topic turned to the crows' flight to Florida, Maisie wanted to know how they happened to be doing such an unusual thing for a flock of crows who normally don't go very far from home and who aren't accustomed to the whole flock flying together. They roost together but fly alone or in pairs.

"Cackle," said Crazy Foot. "She said she'd always wanted to go and was going whether anyone else went or not."

"I did hope you and at least a few others would go, too," said Cackle to Crazy Foot. "When Swooper and then Mamie liked the idea, they helped inspire a lot of those who might not have considered it otherwise. Come to think of it, Swooper is becoming quite a leader."

"Yes, he is," chimed in Lucky and Ruby, who had joined the little group.

"He takes to it naturally," said Ruby. "One day, he'll be head of the council of his own flock." Cackle clicked her agreement.

Meanwhile, some of the younger crows were entertaining themselves with games as they flew along. They played Spot - who could spot various items first. So far, Swooper was the best at that. Tag was one they could all play, although it made their wings tired, having to fly so fast to try to catch someone. Charades were everyone's favorite. Even the little ones who didn't completely understand the game thought it was the best.

In between games, aerial acrobatics kept them occupied. All of them tried loop-de-loops, swoop and dive, and upside-downsies.

Time passed quickly and before they knew it, they were approaching the lighthouse in Hatteras, North Carolina. Cornwell told them to be prepared for occasional very high winds, but not too many tourists this time of the year. As it turned out, both the wind and the sea were calm. Crow cries of delight penetrated the slow-moving air currents as the birds zipped around the lighthouse and explored the parking lot and shoreline nearby.

What's so special about this place?" Asked Budge. "It's just a funny-looking building with stripes painted on it."

"It's a landmark for ships, like all lighthouses," said Cornwell. "They're all quite old now, and some have fallen into disrepair because the ships have other means of guidance. During the Fall hunting season, this is a safe way for us to fly to avoid the hunters. But occasionally, there's a hurricane, or it's so windy that we'd rather go another way."

"Oh," said Budge.

"Let's find something to eat," said Percy.

"Some of the seagrasses are good," said Maisie. "We don't particularly like seagrass," said one of the crows.

"Oh my, oh my," said Maisie. "We didn't think about that!

"What will we do? Cornwell, perhaps we should go somewhere else right now. Cornwell, are "you listening? The crows don't like the grass here. Should we fly inland immediately? Cornie, "Answer me!"

"If you'd stop chattering, I'd try to answer you, dear," said Cornwell. "I suspect our crow friends can tell you better than I what they prefer."

"Most of us are quite eclectic and adventurous when it comes to food," said Lucky, "Although there are a few who can be downright picky. Personally, if I can find a gourmet restaurant, I love to dine on the leftovers. Especially if my goose friends will pardon me, pâté de foie gras. I'll eat basic foods like corn, new corn shoots, worms, and small birds if that's all there is around. I eat a lot."

"What is pâté de foie gras?" said Maisie.

"It's a delicacy made from cooked goose liver," said Lucky. "Sorry."

Maisie shuddered in silence, for once not having anything to say. She knew that people liked to cook and eat goose, but she had never allowed her imagination to consider how.

Everyone within hearing distance slowed down, embarrassed by Lucky's ill-considered remark.

"That could have gone unsaid," said Ruby. "Maisie, please forgive Lucky. We like you, and we're not killers, just omnivorous eaters."

"My favorite is French fries," said Budge.

"Hamburgers with cheese are mine," said Swooper.

"One day, I'll get fat and won't be able to fly because of too much-buttered popcorn," said Percy. His friends laughed at the idea of him so fat he'd have to waddle around on the ground, not flying.

"He'd have to grow extra feathers to cover his fat. Maybe the old feathers would even pop off like a fat man's shirt buttons," said Mamie.

"He'd need a cane to help him walk. Or a walker!" said Penny.

The two geese laughed, too, and Cornwell said, "Of course we forgive Lucky. We know he meant no harm."

Plenty of food was found by all the birds, including a fish caught by Cackle, her first time for sea fishing. The sun, sea air, and full stomachs put the travelers in the mood for an afternoon nap, so it was decided to spend the rest of the day at the mostly deserted beach just south of the lighthouse.

After nap time, the crows played games on the beach while the two geese sat on a small sand dune and watched. They invented a game, something like keep-away, using a large shell until Percy discovered a beach ball. Then, they started a new game of rolling the ball into the water and racing it back when the waves tossed it back. That kept them busy until a breeze sent the ball scooting out on top of the waves. Swooper flew out to get it, but he made a hole in it when he tried to grab it with his beak.

After dinner that evening, they made plans to discuss their route from here in the morning, during, and after breakfast. Then they sat around a driftwood bonfire on the beach and told stories until all the stars in the sky were twinkling their brightest, and everything was still except for the ocean. Even on a calm night, it never stopped its restless pulsing in and out as if it were the heartbeat of the world.

They awoke to loud crashes of waves on the shore. Overnight, everything had changed. Dark clouds had appeared in the sky. The sea was churning with whitecaps and high waves. A storm was brewing, "a nor'easter said Cornwell.

"Ka-ronk, we must be off!" Said Cornwell.

"Caw, caw, caw, caw," sounded the crow alarm, telling them to take to the air quickly.

"Which way?" many of them asked.

"Let's head west away from the sea until we see the first good place to land and discuss our route," said Cornwell. "Good idea," said Crazy Foot, along with several others.

When they were far enough from the offshore wind and saw a place to land, they stopped. After asking some local birds, they discovered that they were near a little town called Jacksonville, North Carolina, which was south and a little west of where they had been. The local birds said that there was a marine base there, Camp Lejeune. "It is where humans, who are a kind of soldiers who protect people in case of attack, come here to train for their work," said one of the locals.

The flock was told that Interstate 95 was an easy route to follow to get to Florida, so they decided to go that way, but knew, because of Cornwell and Maisie's previous trips, that they would have to start going west toward Tampa once they reached the top of Florida. They would have to stop and ask crows, geese, or other birds along the way. Cornwell thought that he and Maisie would start to recognize places they had been before.

Mildred and Gerald once again expressed their concern that they might be in danger of getting off course or away from their intended destination, which had now become the circus, and it is in the vicinity of Tampa instead of Sarasota where it used to be. It has no animals but lots of amazing human acts that involve colorful drama and daredevil athletic feats with costumes galore. The geese who had been there declare that it is well worth the effort to see it.

They say that there are plenty of places for the crows to roost and find food. The whole flock is feeling some excited anticipation for going to the circus because of hearing more and more about it from Cornwell and Maisie. Mildred and Gerald are excited, too, now that they feel quite safe because the two geese are flying along with them.

Before long, they reach I-95, and with it to show them the way, the young ones begin again to think of games to play and songs to sing as they fly along. The winds have subsided, and the sky is clear. Cornwell notices that they are now flying over South Carolina. "What's that?" Swooper asks. "It is a different state from North Carolina," says Cornwell. "What's a state?" asks Mamie.

Cornwell explains that it is one of many specific areas that the country is divided into to manage the people in the various places. That raises more questions that take more answers than Cornwell has. What they understand is that different places have different names and start to look different, too. Some have beaches, and some don't. Some have more trees, buildings, airports, and other things that set them apart. So, they have different names, too. Some have things like the circus. Or at least one place has a circus.

"Oh my, we are seeing and learning so much. This is interesting," says Percy. "I am glad we are going to Florida!"

Soon, Cornwell says to the birds nearby that it looks like they are near Savannah, which is a landmark that tells him he is getting closer to the top of Florida. The birds get excited, especially Swooper and his pals. They chatter and laugh and want to make up a song to celebrate their proximity to Florida. They don't because they get interested in looking below them at the sights of Savannah. It has big squares and parks and weird-looking stringy stuff hanging from trees. They are told by Maisie that it is called Spanish Moss. They are still above I-95 and keeping an eye out for the highway that goes toward Tampa. Cornwell says that it is not far from the beginning of Florida. "As soon as we see Jacksonville, we are in Florida," says Cornwell.

"What shall we sing now?" Asks Mamie to no one in particular. Swooper starts making up words to a song about "J, J, J Jacksonville, Jumpin' Jacksonville." he sings, if you can call his voice singing. The others laugh about his lack of a tune. Then someone shouts out,

"St. Augustine! Isn't that where the famous fountain is?" "Yes, the famous fountain that was discovered by a human, Ponce de Leon, in the 1500's", answered Cornwell again. He clearly seems to be the knowledgeable one.

Before anyone knows it, they are right above highway 4, the one that goes to Tampa. Cornwell recognizes some landmarks. "Cornwell, I would like to stop for a little break since we are now on the last leg of this trip," says Maisie. "Of course, dear," he replies. "Let's find a good place to alight for a bit," he announces to the group.

"Good idea, yes, ok…" are the replies as birds start to fly low, looking for landing spots on what is a very firm-looking beach. The beach is Daytona, known for being the site of the International Speedway and its famous auto race. Also known for its sand, so firm in some places that it supports autos driving on it.

"Whew, it feels good to stop," says Penny, echoed by several cries of "You can say that again" and "for sure," and "Yes, it does."

Crazy Foot turns to Cackle and says, "It sounds as if a lot of the group are glad for a rest. I wonder if, when we take off from here, we should actively be looking for a place to stop for the night. What do you think?"

"I think that is a good suggestion. Why don't we ask everyone?" says Cackle.

Crazy Foot decides to ask Cornwell if he thinks that looking for a spot is possible here and if he thinks it is a good idea. Cornwell agrees. "I think it is a very good idea," he says, "And, yes, I think we can find a place nearby. I can't at the moment remember a place near here, but once we are back in the air, something is bound to look familiar."

Cackle calls for everyone to listen up that Crazy Foot has something to suggest. "Let's find a place to stop and chat."

There's a hubbub as all the flock starts looking for a place.

"I see a nice spot with a few trees and some sort of mounds of sand," says Swooper. "Look down and to your right." Comments agreeing with him, "Oh yes, that looks good," and "Oh sure, let's go investigate," and more. One by one, the flock is together on this sandy spot that is somewhere closer and closer to Tampa.

Cackle says, "Cornwell and Crazy Foot are thinking that several comments have been made about how nice it was to take a break, and some are tired from flying so long that maybe we should start looking for a place to roost for the night. We want to know if you think that's a good idea."

There's a general agreement as the smaller groups chat about looking for a spot. Percy speaks up, saying that he and his friends, Mamie, Swooper, Penny, and more, all agree. They also concur that most of them are feeling tired, too.

Ruby pipes up and says that she thinks it is a terrific idea and that she is ready to stop as soon as they find a good place.

"Well," Cornwell says, "since it seems that most of us agree it is time to look, I want to say that I have no certain memory of a place nearby, but that if we rest a short while and then when we take off again, I suspect and hope that I recognize some of this territory and that might help jog my memory. After all, I am getting to be an older gander and don't remember every single part of this flight."

"Here here, says Lucky; thanks go to Cornwell! We are so glad you and Maisie are with us!"

"Shall we rest a bit more and then fly up to start looking for a roost?" Says Cackle.

Cries of "Ok" and "Yes!" make a joyful noise of happiness.

With such hopeful intentions, the flock begins to take off for the air again. They are flying above Rt 4, the one that is taking them from Daytona to Tampa. Soon, Cornwell tells Cackle and Crazy Foot this this area looks familiar. He knows there is a lake nearby and a zoo. Those around him start to get excited, and then they spot the lake. They are somewhere over Orlando. The feeling is one many travelers experience when they know they are near their destination. Cornwell suggests they wait to get past this congested city area. He thinks there will be good roosting places beyond it. Sure enough, they spot another small lake and some open areas that look likely. There are trees, grass, and fields. When Cornwell sees what looks like a small forest of various trees, he muses that it looks like a good place to find somewhere to spend the night. Cackle lets the flock know that it is time to fly closer and begin to seriously look for a place to roost. Cries of "yay" and "all right!" issue from the flock as they begin to actively investigate and see another lake.

They stop on the ground near the lake and quickly meet some robins and then a pair of woodpeckers who are very curious as to what this whole group of crows is doing there. They ask and are told by Cornwell about their intention to fly to Tampa. The local birds say that Tampa is a short flight away to the west and that, yes, this little area near Lake Alfred would be a good place to find food and a roost for the night.

The flock picks a group of trees that look good and begins foraging for food, very excited to be so close to Tampa. There is a lot of chatter about Tampa and the circus.

"Do you think we could be in the circus?" Said Percy. "We could do a lot of flying loop de loops and stuff like that! Wouldn't that be fun!" His friends get a laugh out of thinking about that.

Let's think about what we might say to the ones who run the circus, says Swooper. "Good idea", says Penny.

"First, for example, what do we know about what happens at the circus?" Says Swooper.

"Maisie said that there are acrobats and tightrope walkers," Percy says.

"What are tightrope walkers and acrobats?" Asks Penny. "Let's ask Cornwell and Maisie since they have been there!"

Swooper, Penny, and Percy go to find Maisie and Cornwell to ask them about the circus. They find them resting near the little lake. "Maisie and Cornwell, may we ask you some questions about the circus?" Swooper says

"Hi there, Swooper, Penny, and Percy!" Says Cornwell. "Of course, you may ask us about the circus! What do you want to know?"

"Well, we were wondering," says Percy, "if we might be able to participate in it. But first, we need to know what the performers do. Like, what are acrobats and tightrope walkers?"

Cornwell chuckles and then says, "Well, let me see. Tightrope walkers are people who walk along a rope that is set high above the ground between two poles that are upright inside the circus tent. They must have a good balance in order to do that. Sometimes, they hold onto a long, skinny pole that helps them balance. But you birds would have no trouble with that. Your wings would help you stay on the rope! Acrobats, on the other hand, do all sorts of things that are athletic and show their skills at jumping, leaping, balancing on each other and things like that. Things that wow the spectators."

"I bet we could wow the spectators, too!" Says Percy.

"Yes, yes," said Penny and Swooper, almost in unison.

"I bet you could, too," says Maisie. "Why don't you put your heads together and think of some things to ask the circus leaders when we get there."

"Let's do!" says Penny, with nods from Swooper and Percy.

All the birds, but especially the younger ones, are getting both curious about the circus and more and more excited to be on the way to seeing it. And maybe even finding ways to participate in it. The Circus has become the destination for this trip.

About the Author

 Mary Lamb Lucas started writing when she was eight years old, inspired by having had the book Little House on the Prairie read to her whole third grade class. She wanted to write her own version of it. She finished her schooling, including college, with some writing classes along the way. Then she married and became the mother of five wonderful children. She read to them, helped them grow, wrote some columns in the local newspaper, introduced the kids to her love of horses, and eventually wrote what became her first book. Cackle Goes to Florida is her second book.